Pebble®

Families

Sisters

by Lola M. Schaefer

Consulting Editor: Gail Saunders-Smith, PhD

Capstone
press®

Mankato, Minnesota

D1125706

Pebble Books are published by Capstone Press,
151 Good Counsel Drive, P.O. Box 669, Mankato, Minnesota 56002.
www.capstonepub.com

Books published by Capstone Press are manufactured with paper
containing at least 10 percent post-consumer waste.

Library of Congress Cataloging-in-Publication Data
Schaefer, Lola M., 1950–
    Sisters/by Lola M. Schaefer. — Rev. and updated ed.
    p. cm. — (Pebble books. Families)
    Summary: "Simple text and photographs present sisters and how they interact with
their families" — Provided by publisher.
    Includes bibliographical references and index.
    ISBN-13: 978-1-4296-1228-9 (hardcover)   ISBN-10: 1-4296-1228-2 (hardcover)
    ISBN-13: 978-1-4296-1757-4 (softcover)   ISBN-10: 1-4296-1757-8 (softcover)
    1. Sisters — Juvenile literature. I. Title. II. Series.
HQ759.96.S33 2008
306.875'4 — dc22   2007027100

Note to Parents and Teachers

The Families set supports national social studies standards related
to identifying family members and their roles in the family. This
book describes and illustrates sisters. The images support early
readers in understanding the text. The repetition of words and
phrases helps early readers learn new words. This book also
introduces early readers to subject-specific vocabulary words, which
are defined in the glossary section. Early readers may need some
assistance to read some words and to use the Table of Contents,
Glossary, Read More, Internet Sites, and Index sections of the book.

Printed in the United States of America in Stevens Point, Wisconsin.
072012   006841CPS

Table of Contents

Sisters

Sisters are girls
who have the same parents
as other children.

brother

mother

sister

father

Sisters have brothers.

Sisters have sisters.

Sisters Work

Sisters work together.
Megan and her sister
dry dishes.

Julie and her brother build a fort.

At Play

Sisters play.

Kate and her brother swing.

Amanda and her brother dress up.

Teresa and her sister
fly a kite.

Irma teaches her little brother a new game.

Sisters smile.

Glossary

brother — a boy or a man who has the same parents as another person

fort — a building or structure to play in; a fort can be on the ground or built up in a tree.

parent — a mother or a father of one child or many children; when a parent has more than one child, the children are called siblings.

teach — to show someone how to do something; older siblings often teach younger siblings new things as they grow up.

Read More

Dwight, Laura. *Brothers and Sisters.* New York: Star Bright Books, 2005.

Katz, Karen. *Best-Ever Big Sister.* Lift-the-Flap Book. New York: Grosset & Dunlap, 2006.

Internet Sites

FactHound offers a safe, fun way to find Internet sites related to this book. All of the sites on FactHound have been researched by our staff.

Here's how:

1. Visit *www.facthound.com*
2. Choose your grade level.
3. Type in this book ID **1429612282** for age-appropriate sites. You may also browse subjects by clicking on letters, or by clicking on pictures and words.
4. Click on the **Fetch It** button.

FactHound will fetch the best sites for you!

Index

Word Count: 63
Grade 1
Early-Intervention Level: 10

Editorial Credits
Sarah L. Schuette, revised edition editor; Kim Brown, revised edition designer

Photo Credits
Capstone Press/Karon Dubke, all